THE RENAISSANCE

A History From Beginning to End

BY

HENRY FREEMAN

Table of Contents

How Art, Science, Technology, and Religion Helped Europe Deliver a Rebirth of the Human Spirit

The Middle Ages saw Europe forge a new identity as a collection of individual nations, no longer part of the fallen Roman Empire, that developed their own ethnic character.

During the Middle Ages, the nations of Europe forged new identities that moved them away from the lost glory of the Roman Empire into their own ethnicity. The experience of maturation was often clumsy and out of step, an evolutionary process that saw the nation's developing at their own pace as they struggled to replace the protection of Rome with their own home-grown strength. What the nations, once they were ready to be described in that manner, did have was the Roman Catholic Church, which defined itself as the spiritual protector of Christian believers. But the dutiful Christians of the Middle Ages who sought orthodoxy and for the most part obeyed the papal rules underwent a change when the Middle Ages ended. The Renaissance, or rebirth, was a period of time when Europeans began to question what they had been told was sacrosanct. Through art, inventions, science, literature, and theology, the separate nations of the European continent sought answers that the Roman Catholic Church was unwilling, or perhaps unable, to offer. The Church that had become a powerful political entity was viewed with distrust and skepticism by many Christians; the spread of learning that accompanied the invention of Gutenberg's printing press meant that bold new ideas were traveling across the boundaries of Europe faster than the Church could silence them. Lascivious, power-brokering popes could not bring a halt to the challenges they encountered when a German priest rebelled against corrupt practices that masqueraded as ecclesiastical authority. As the walls came tumbling down, humanism burst forth, inspiring the art of Michelangelo, the science of Vesalius, the literature of Shakespeare and Cervantes. But with the loss of religious uniformity came terrible conflicts: France suffered the St. Bartholomew's Day Massacre; Spain welcomed the Inquisition to purge heresy; the Low Countries were split between Catholic and Protestant. The Renaissance was a triumph of the human spirit and a confirmation of human ability, even as it affirmed the willingness of men and women to die for the right to think freely.

Chapter One

The Rebirth of Europe

During the Middle Ages, unquestioning faith was the order of the day, and questions had little place in society. But those questions which had been dormant before the Renaissance suddenly burst forth to interpret a new lexicon of observations that would lead to answers based on fact rather than faith. The physical world excited brilliant minds who engaged in experimentation to answer the unsolved mysteries of nature. Leonardo da Vinci did not confine his abilities to his art brush: he studied the anatomy of the human body, not simply as an artist, but by dissecting cadavers, an act forbidden by the Roman Catholic Church. His creativity could not be contained by canvas, as he foretold the future of war by designing machines that could fly and sail underwater. For da Vinci, it was not enough to see what was there; he envisioned what could be there in times to come.

How did Galileo learn that objects fall at the same rate of acceleration? He dropped cannon balls of varying sizes from the top of a building. How did he determine that the Earth was not the center of the universe, and that the Earth, along with the other planets, paid homage to the sun by revolving around it? He built a telescope that proved his premise. His bold discovery, which contradicted the teachings of the Church and its view that the Earth was the center of the universe, brought him into conflict with the Church hierarchy, earning him the label of heretic and a sentence of house arrest because he would not recant his belief. But how could he? The telescope had shown him the truth.

Learning, which once had been doled out in small, rationed doses to a privileged few because it could not be disseminated to many was, in the Renaissance, accelerated. That's because in 1440, Johannes Gutenberg invented the mechanical moving type printing press that could print books quickly, in comparison to the laborious copying process which had confined the sharing of knowledge. Machines began to do the work that had depended on human labor and as men and women gained precious hours, their interest in literacy and learning could grow. But as the Renaissance would demonstrate, learning was a double-edged sword because with knowledge came questions that the Church could not answer and would not tolerate. The Inquisition would address the problem of questions which violated the teachings of the Church and instead of becoming martyrs, the Church would create them.

Chapter Two

The Italian Renaissance

Once upon a time, Rome was an Empire and the lands it contained were regional entities which had pre-imperial pasts followed by inclusion within the Empire, a status generally achieved by the power of the Roman legions but which was eventually accepted by the subject nations. Then Rome fell and the nations, untethered to a central authority, were obliged to discern for themselves who they were as part of the Europe.

For most of Europe, the cities were important, but subordinate to the countries in which they were located. Italy reversed that process with independent city-states. The Papal States, located in Rome and the northeastern Italian peninsula, were ostensibly the church hierarchy entrusted with the care of the spiritual domain, but in truth they were powerful administrators intent on expanding their political base. Venice and Florence were republics that were controlled by nobles and budding capitalists with wealth that arose from trade rather than family inheritance. Naples was a kingdom and Milan was a duchy. There was no illusion that, collectively, they were Italy, but in their own right, they held sway over commerce, trade, arts, and power in Europe.

Wealth was changing the demographic of power. The bankers were not aristocrats, but their acquisition of wealth meant that wealth was being redistributed. From a time when power was based on the ownership of land by the wellborn, commercial advances saw wealth shift to people who did not have a pedigree of birth. The bankers had the money and the nobility needed it. The nobles were not accustomed to having to preserve their acquisitions or to acquire more, and they relied on banking loans to fund their wars and their lifestyles. By the end of the 15th century, the nobles who had defaulted on their loans had lost their wealth to the commercial powers. A new power structure was forming.

Approximately one-fourth to one-third of the population was poor. There were also slaves during this time, the first attempt in post-classical Europe to consider slavery as an economic option. Merchants and tradespeople—small businessmen in today's lexicon— were the next layer of social strata, beneath the bankers who were beginning to emerge as power brokers because of their control of wealth and their support of capitalism. On the top of the social structure were the traditional nobility class and the merchant class that dominated the cities.

The brilliant minds of the Renaissance rediscovered their ancient roots and with the rebirth of interest in Greek and Roman learning, the Renaissance, rooting itself in its lost heritage, built a new philosophy which bypassed the ecclesiastical formula of asceticism to discover worldly pleasures: beauty and the intellect became the new lodestars of a population that looked to its own talents and awareness to define the world.

Papal power and nepotism were joined at the hip as the popes of the Renaissance transformed the papacy into a family business. The man who became Pope Julius II in 1503 was himself the nephew of Pope Sixtus IV, and was elected at the age of 18 to the College of Cardinals in 1471. He was an advisor to Pope Innocent VIII. Whether or not the authenticity of his spirituality could be questioned, there was no doubt about his diplomatic network. He served on two diplomatic missions to France that promoted the involvement of the French in Italian affairs. The popes were intent on preserving power in a worldly domain that had very little in common with poverty, chastity, or obedience.

Its early start did not bestow longevity upon the Italian Renaissance. Other nations eventually caught up, and by the time the 15th century came to a close, Italy was torn by war. The Roman Catholic Church was fighting ruthlessly against a culture of dissent which had breathed the free air of thought unencumbered by the chains of faith. Scandal and corruption tainted the Holy See. Other European countries, France, Spain, England, wanted to plunder the city-states. They were not alone: the Pope wanted the same thing, and the Holy Roman Emperor also had designs on the lands. When the Roman Inquisition was established in 1545, independent thought became an invitation to heresy. Without questioning, the Renaissance was stifled. The Inquisition would spread its influence and its terror into the Catholic countries which were determined to douse all traces of what it regarded as heresy. But as the Renaissance promulgated free thought, it was harder for the Church to control the thoughts of the faithful. Minds searching for truth were less fearful of the threat of excommunication, which had been the Church's most persuasive weapon to keep its flock in line.

The Italian City-States

After the fall of the Roman Empire, the geographical landscape of Italy didn't evolve into a nation. Rather, the peninsula formed independent republics or city-states. The jewel of them all was Florence, a powerful commercial center with the third largest population in Europe after London and Constantinople.

With money and influence, it was a natural evolution for Florentines to celebrate their affluence, and as the focus of existence changed from the survival and faith ethos of the Middle Ages, a new humanism began to emerge. Culture was a new index of wealth and Florentines who emerged as art patrons found a thriving pool of talent to support.

Florence: The Incubator of the Renaissance

It's fitting that an Italian city should be credited as the birthplace of the Renaissance. Rome at its height had sponsored Europe's safety and prosperity until the mounting success of barbarian invasions by the Vandals, Goths, Ostrogoths, etc. so weakened the Empire that by 476, when the Emperor Romulus Augustulus was deposed and Odoacer become the King of Italy, there was no hope of resurrecting imperial authority. That left Europe on its own. Rome was, however, the seat of power for the Christian Church, and the spiritual authority of the Church would, in time, rival the imperial might of its predecessor.

The Middle Ages were a complicated period of time which saw Europe arise from a motley assortment of feeble nations into a powerful and vibrant political landscape. By the year 1450, which is generally regarded as the opening year of the Renaissance, Europe had seen the rise of the monarchy, the advances of technology, the weakening of feudalism, and the omnipotence of the Christian Church. But it had also endured famine and plague which reduced the Continent's population by as much as 40 percent. A series of conflicts between England and France had given birth to the Hundred Years' War. Joan of Arc would be burned at the stake by the English and canonized by the Pope for her defense of the realm of France. Charlemagne would create an empire that would be lost by his heirs. Kings mindful of their own ignorance and lamenting their lack of knowledge would support the growth of learning.

By the end of the Renaissance, the medieval mindset was no more, the dominance if the church was tested by the rise of science, and the growth of representative government would gradually alter the balance of power and the concept of the monarchy.

Power consumed those who sought it. But the arts enlightened those who enjoyed it, and the Renaissance was flush with artists whose talent made their worlds a living canvas.

Art in the Italian Renaissance

For architect Filippo Brunelleschi, the designs of classical Rome inspired his own work. The Santa Maria del Fiore

Cathedral in Florence, with its eight-sided dome, was regarded as a masterpiece of the new engineering which used no buttresses to support its 37,000-ton weight. As was the case with other Renaissance standouts, Brunelleschi didn't merely design buildings. He was a painter as well, one who altered the way in which art was recreated. His painting used linear perspective so that he painted from the viewer's point of view, allowing the space to recede into the frame. However, the concept of linear perspective which Brunelleschi employed to such success belonged to another architect, Leon Battista Alberti, whose work On Painting was adopted by other artists. Later, the illusion of three-dimensional space on a flat canvas would exemplify a new technique called chiaroscuro.

Creative minds both shared what they discovered and competed to be the very best at using it. Did the Italian Renaissance begin as an early rendition of "Renaissance Idol" in 1401, when Lorenzo Ghiberti and Filippo Brunelleschi were in a competition to build the bronze doors for the Florence Cathedral's Baptistery? Ghiberti won, but Brunelleschi was never an also-ran. Artists continued to compete for commissions, and with a collection of competitors such as Donatello and Masaccio, the ultimate winners would be posterity.

RENAISSANCE MAN: Michelangelo

Michelangelo Buonarroti, like many of his contemporaries, was a hyphenate: a sculptor-painter-architect whose creative works show a level of physical realism that ignited the Renaissance. That level of talent was sought after by the power elite of patrons, including the Catholic Church. In his youth, his determination to become an artist did not meet with his family's blessing, but Michelangelo persevered and finally his father gave way and apprenticed his 14-year-old son to an artist in Florence. His father's capitulation would be rewarded by the ultimate results of success, but Michelangelo would have his share of enemies as well as patrons. Michelangelo's rivals in Rome's artist colony, which included Raphael, and St. Peters architect Donato Bramante, were jealous of his prowess, so they devised a plot to bring him down.

Pope Julius II wanted to have the ceiling in the Sistine Chapel in the Vatican painted. Why not get the Pope to offer the brash sculptor, who had never done a fresco, the commission? When he failed, as they were sure he would, he would be disgraced. Michelangelo was unwilling to take the assignment, but the Pope pressed him. The assignment proved to be grueling; Michelangelo painted on top of scaffolding so that he could be close enough to his work. Throughout the process, the artist and the Pope battled over the outcome; Four years after he began, his work was done and his scheming rivals were vanquished by the results.

Although pope and artist squabbled fiercely, their conflict was over art. The time was coming when disagreement with a church leader could lead to much more serious consequences.

Chapter Three

The French Renaissance

Italy may have been an early bloomer in the Renaissance, but it wouldn't be long before other European nations would feel the stirrings of rebirth. The French, by invading Italy in 1494, helped to bring an end to the Italian Renaissance while ushering in the Renaissance for France; the tenure for the time period is often timed from the 1492 invasion under King Charles VIII to the death of Henry IV in 1610. The Middle Ages had taken its toll; France, as well as the other European countries, had greatly suffered from the bubonic plague of the 1340s and the Hundred Years War with England, which didn't end until 1453.

Religion in Renaissance France

As Europe split into Catholic and Protestant factions, national policies reflected loyalties which claimed to come from religious loyalty but were no strangers to secular options. Catherine de Medici, the widow of Henry II, was an extremely powerful influence during the reigns of her sons Francis II, Charles IX, and Henry III. Marrying her Catholic daughter to the Protestant Henry of Navarre seemed like an expedient compromise between the established Catholic faith and the new beliefs which were becoming more prevalent. But Queen Catherine was doubtful that one country could nurture two such opposite beliefs and maintain peace, and peace was what she desired. She was willing to go to almost any lengths to preserve peace on her terms.

On the night before the wedding, on St. Bartholomew's Day, August 24, 1572, the order was given to kill the Huguenots (French Protestants). The bloody event is known as the St. Bartholomew's Day Massacre. War in France ensued; Henry of Navarre went to war against France's King Henry III and French nobleman Henry de Guise. The war became known as the War of the Three Henrys. But ultimately, only one Henry remained. After both Henry of Guise and King Henry III died, Henry of Navarre, deciding that Paris was worth a mass, converted to Catholicism and became the king. Henry IV's Edict of Nantes granted religious peace to both Catholics and Protestants in France, encouraging tolerance between the factions. However, those deep divisions could not be erased, and in 1610, Henry was assassinated by a Roman Catholic.

Music in Renaissance France

As was the case with so many of the Renaissance arts, even music took sides in religion. For Catholics, the Latin motet was the preferred style of sacred music, but the Protestant sound was very different. Each side created a variation of the chanson spirituelle, which resembled a secular song with a religious text. Music would claim its martyrs in the religious wars that were in danger of severing France; the Protestant composer Claude Goudimel was killed during the St. Bartholomew's Day

Massacre. In 1581, a Catholic composer, Antoine de Bertrand, was slain by Protestants.

But music remained a cherished part of French culture, and it was in the area of music that the French influence in the Renaissance was most noted. King Francis I brought musicians with him when he traveled, and one of the competitions that took place when he met England's King Henry VIII at the Field of the Cloth of Gold was for the best musical entertainment.

The chanson, a secular song for three or four voices, became one of the most popular musical forms of the 16th century. Composer Clement Janequin composed La guerre which was written in honor of the 1515 victory of France at Marignano. The song evokes trumpets to sound retreat and advance, the sounds of the wounded, and the cannon. The inspiration for the musical form came from Ancient Greece, but the movement was also showing up in Italy, where it was known as the Florentine Camerata.

For the French, the allure of music was the peaceful part of the Renaissance, a time when human creativity sometimes took a back seat to the fervor of human religious convictions that, too often, ended in bloodshed.

Chapter Four

The Spanish Renaissance

The story is told that, In 711, a Muslim governor in North Africa answered the request of a Christian leader who sought his help against the Visigoth tyrant named Roderick who ruled Spain. The governor sent an army of 7000 troops under the command of a general named Tariq bin Ziyad; they landed at a place which they named Jabal At-Tariq, or "Rock of Tariq" after the general, but later generations would call the landing site Gibraltar. Whether or not the invasion truly came about as a result of a request by a Christian is not confirmed, but what is certain is that the Visigoths were defeated, Roderick was killed, and by 720, Spain was in the hands of the Moors, as Muslims were known at the time.

That time of Islamic rule would leave traces upon the Iberian Peninsula, until Isabella of Castile and Ferdinand of Aragon, Christian monarchs committed to the unification of Spain and the authority of the Catholic Church, forced the Muslims to leave Granada, the remaining kingdom which had been under Muslim control until 1492 when the Spanish armies were victorious. Spain would be united and Spain would be Christian.

The married monarchs who joined Castile and Aragon also joined forces to create a new political paradigm; their format was to strengthen the executive power of the monarchy by making strategic alliances with the influential families of their realm to transform the monarchy into the center of power. The aristocracy was certainly a player in the power structure, but the monarchs ruled.

For Spain, 1492 was a year of record. It's regarded as the beginning of the Spanish Renaissance; of course, it's also the year when Christopher Columbus of Genoa sailed for the New World with the blessing and financial support of the Spanish monarchs, Isabella and Ferdinand. Spain would grow in land and wealth and influence as a result of the explorations it sponsored, but within its internal borders, dissension was heresy.

In the either/or world of faith, a believer was a Christian and anyone else was an infidel. Spain's rigid Roman Catholic beliefs shaped the course of its Renaissance, and in 1478, the Inquisition was introduced, a weapon in the arsenal of the Church which would become notorious and which would affect Spain's history.

RELIGION IN THE SPANISH RENAISSANCE

Religion was changing in Renaissance Europe. The church, still powerful, was thoroughly engaged in secular politics. But as new ideas permeated the membrane of ecclesiastical hierarchy, some concepts came not from the upper levels but from the lower ones. Bartolome de las Casas, a Dominican friar, actually opposed forcing indigenous peoples of the New World to convert to Christianity because, he felt, force was the antithesis of both Christian precepts and the nature of mortal men and woman. Colonialism and its brutality were not in harmony with the humanism that the Renaissance espoused.

The rise of the Reformation led to a religious response as the Counterreformation got underway. Catholic leaders gathered in 1545 in Trent to, as they saw it, protect the purity of their doctrine from the heresy of Protestantism. They established standards for monastic reform and priestly chastity, as well as orthodoxy. The Jesuits were formed under the authority of Ignatius Loyola to support the church. The Council named 583 books it deemed as heretical, including the writings of Luther, Calvin, and Erasmus, as well as most translations of the Bible. But the church did emulate some of the new methods of the Reformation, with the building of new churches which could accommodate many more worshippers designed with acoustics for sermons in the native tongues of the worshippers. The Council adopted the practice of the Inquisition which the Spaniards had introduced in order to stamp out dissent. For a transgressor who was reported to the local Inquisitor, one's innocence had to be proven because guilt was assumed and torture in the name of God was sanctioned.

RENAISSANCE WOMAN: St. Theresa of Avila

Religion had long been an area where women could make their mark throughout the Middle ages, and this did not end with the Renaissance. One female mystic, Teresa Ali Fatim Corella Sanchez de Cepeda y Ahumada, brought her religious passion and spirit of reform to the Catholic Church. Daughters of that time were expected to be dutiful, but Teresa recognized her obligation to her divine father. At the age of seven, she wanted to be a martyr and was on her way to seek decapitation from the Muslims when her uncle discovered what she was doing and brought her back home. Her mother died when she was 14 years old, but Teresa shared her mother's love of reading fiction, a trait which concerned her father, who regarded her rebellious nature and her youthful fondness for frivolities like clothing and flirting as signs of trouble, and sent her to a convent at the age of 16. She was not sure that she had a true vocation, and struggled when it was time to choose between the convent and marriage. She became a Carmelite nun but found her prayer life lacking inspiration as she noticed that some of the other nuns seemed devoid of a religious vocation. The convent was a place to put women who didn't fit into society and not all women were spiritually inclined.

The dearth of spirituality troubled Teresa. Illness fell upon her, including malaria, paralysis, and seizures. She was so ill that a grave was dug for her, but she recovered, although she continued to suffer, as did her prayer life. At the age of 41, she was still susceptible to distractions that intruded upon her prayers. Then she realized that her understanding of prayer needed to evolve Prayer, she said, was an intimate sharing between friends, and taking time to be alone with God. It was loving, not thinking, that was the key. Newly invigorated by spirituality, she would have episodes of religious ecstasy when she prayed, overcome by her love for God. Her friends were concerned when they saw her devotion to God rather than worldly friendships as demonic possession, but when she was analyzed by a Jesuit, he confirmed that she was inspired by God and not the devil.

When she was 43, she sought to found a convent that was based upon the contemplative life of poverty, prayer and simplicity. But she received condemnation and criticism for this decision and was even threatened with litigation from the town where the Carmelite convent to which she belonged was located. Nonetheless, she founded St. Josephs and spent much time in writing, but she still attracted controversy. However when the Inquisition investigated her, they found her innocent of sin. At age 51, she decided to spread her movement to found more convents based upon her reforms. In order to avoid a riot, she would enter towns covertly and late at night. Her vows were to God, not to the nobility and when a princess who wanted to enter the convent Teresa had founded expected the other nuns to serve her on their knees, Teresa objected. The princess was outraged and again the Inquisition was called in to investigate the charges. But her sincerity, combined with the publicity which actually served her in good stead, let to a growing interest among women wanting to join her convents. Her novel notions about prayer fascinated the faithful and Europe and crossed the borders of Spain into other countries. She died at the age of 67 after being commanded by an archbishop, despite her illness, to attend to the birth of a noblewoman.

Much of the Renaissance drew inspiration from new ideas that altered art, literature, science and the social order, but the radical ideas of a Catholic nun also revolutionized prayer.

THE ARTS OF THE SPANISH RENAISSANCE

In common with France, the Spanish imported their artists, bringing in Italians and sending Spanish apprentices to be trained in the new style. The artist Titian was commissioned to paint for Spanish patrons, but he didn't move to Spain to work.

One hybrid style was to blend Granada's Nasrid art with Flemish influences to create a form of painting which, although based on tradition but reflected the new Renaissance touch. The patronage of King Charles I was able to achieve a Spanish Renaissance flavor in its art; artists such as Pedro Berruguete, Juane de Juanes and Paolo da San Leocadio displayed quality and skill in their works.

The first grammar book in any of the Romance languages was written by a Spaniard, Antonio de Nebrija, who published Gramatica Castellana in 1492, another reason why the year was memorable. It was at this time that Latin was replaced by Castilian as the official language of Spain. Under King Charles I, the Spaniards were able to enter the Renaissance with some freedom, but during the reign of Philip II, religion and the Inquisition overruled the dynamism of the Renaissance's potential to blossom.

RENAISSANCE MAN: Miguel De Cervantes

In 1547, the man who is regarded as the author of the first modern European novel went to Rome at the age of 22 to work for either a cardinal or a nobleman (accounts differ). He left that position to become a soldier. He was fighting against the Turks in 1571 when his left hand was wounded, requiring a lengthy time to recover. He rejoined the soldier's life in 1572, but in 1575, he and his brother were captured by Barbary pirates. They were imprisoned in Algiers for five years until a ransom raised by his father and a Catholic religious order was paid to buy his freedom. When he returned home, he was a poor man who needed an income, but the years of captivity would prove lucrative in their own way. His time as a prisoner, although a time of personal suffering, served as an inspiration for his creativity as his writing would explore the concept of freedom and captivity. In 1582, he re-enlisted in the army but in 1583 when he returned to Spain, he had a manuscript with him. Around this time, he also became the father of a daughter born to a member of the Portuguese nobility.

Although he was writing at this time, his income came from his work as a tax collector for the Spanish government. Finances were a problem and Cervantes ended up in jail in 1597. But in 1605, the publication of the first segment of Don Quixote made him a writer.

From 1607 until his death nine years later, he continued to write, establishing a reputation for his literary work and a lasting legacy for his leadership in literature.

Chapter Five

The German Renaissance

Germany's Renaissance was getting underway as the Italian Renaissance was ending, but German innovation would play a powerful role in that demise. Germany entered the 16th century as one of the most prosperous of European countries. Although it lacked the urban growth that was seen in the Italian Renaissance, Germany could boast of industries such as metallurgy and mining, textiles and banking. But the invention of the printing press by Johannes Gutenberg in 1440 would eventually prove to be the intellectual engine of the Renaissance, driving new ideas, some of them radical, across the Continent as books were more readily available. The printing press would itself nurture another commercial enterprise which the Germans would master as German printers dominated the field well into the 16th century.

Disgust with the corruption of the Catholic Church fostered a spirit of rebellion in Germany, especially against the sale of indulgences which the papal powers used to raise money by placing a price on the forgiveness of sins. The growth of humanism had already dealt the Church a blow by the enthusiastic examination of ancient historical documents which refuted numerous Church teachings. In a world where unilateral church authority was autocratic and unquestioned, that intellectual dissent would not have thrived, or perhaps would not even have gained momentum. But by the time of the German

Renaissance in the fifteenth century, the church was exposed for its own sins.

Without the invention of the printing press, the seismic changes that transformed Europe would have been stalled. The Italian Renaissance, although it was an avatar of the changes that bubbled up from the Middle Ages, led to a new focus on the human, rather than the spiritual, sphere of knowledge. Ultimately that unique vision would bring a searing examination of the Catholic Church, the power-grabbing Popes and the Church hierarchy which brokered more in politics than in souls.

A German priest named Martin Luther had traveled to Italy and witnessed the worldly lifestyles of the Roman Catholic Church hierarchy. He saw how the sale of indulgences, which offered forgiveness for a fee, was used to finance a new St. Peter's basilica. The momentum for change had begun earlier and Protestantism was not entirely new, but buoyed by the volcanic thrust of intellectual inspiration that emerged from the Renaissance, a Reformation was empowered to challenge the church and bring change. The Renaissance had seen the behavior of popes come to increasingly parallel the behavior of princes, as they attempted to compete with the gilded city-states around them.

RENAISSANCE MAN: Martin Luther

The papacy did not expect the political leaders of Europe to challenge religious authority. In 1517, Luther published his Ninety-five Theses and indicted the Catholic Church for its corrupt practices which defrauded the spirit of the original gospels. To the disbelief of Pope Leo, the German rulers did not buckle; instead, they declared that they were not subject to the rule of the Vatican. Their defiance saved Luther's life.

Luther also believed that biblical knowledge should be available in the languages of its believers and he translated the Bible into German so that ordinary people could read the Holy Scriptures and understand it.

Technology in Renaissance Germany

With the ability to mass produce printed materials, a new medium would emerge: the newspaper. With the accessibility of printed works and a new emphasis on literacy and education, more people wanted to find out more about the events of their societies. The previously circulated handwritten newsprints were not satisfactory, and in 1605, Strassburg's Johann Carolus published his newssheet with the aid of a printing press. The popularity of the concept spread to Basel, Frankfurt, and Berlin, which also used the printing press to publish German-language newspapers. The news was not only a popular topic for reading in Germany; by the mid-1600s, approximately one-quarter of the population of the Holy Roman Empire was literate and reading the political newspapers.

RENAISSANCE MAN: Johannes Gutenberg

Twenty-first-century society sees mass communication in terms of computers, cell phones, and mobile devices. For

Renaissance Europe, there was only one form of mass communication but it was sufficient to transform a continent. The names of Jobs, Gates, and Zuckerberg are instantly recognizable today as the titans of technology who have redefined communication and commerce, but, extensive though their influence is, they pale before the innovation of their predecessor, who changed the world.

The name Gutenberg, which means Beautiful Mountain, is synonymous with the invention of the printing press, but Johannes Gensfleisch zur Laden (which translates to Gooseflesh) didn't just create a technological revolution, he advanced civilization as new ideas spread faster and broader. Thanks to the printing press, concepts which challenged the status quo were no longer the sole province of the elite.

Born in 1399 to an affluent family, young Johann was taught to read. At that time, handwritten manuscripts had been replaced by block-printing: the printer cut a page-sized block of hardwood and cut out the individual words of writing upon the block. He then cut away the wood from the sides of the letters, leaving the letters raised. Ink was applied, paper was placed upon the block and pressed down. It was faster than hand-copying, but it was still time-consuming. Gutenberg, who loved to read, felt that it was unfortunate that only the rich could afford books and he began to explore ways to change that fact.

He moved to the city of Strassburg where he was not known and found a room in an abandoned monastery to use for a workshop. During the day he worked on his secret invention, experimenting with ways to speed up the printing process. He ran out of funds before his experiment yield results, but when a Mainz goldsmith and lawyer named Johann Fust became interested in Gutenberg's plans, he decided it was worthwhile to become the young man's patron, loaning him 800 guilders to establish a plant and buy the tools he needed. Experimenting continued and when Gutenberg switched from wooden to metal type, he made more progress. But not fast enough; Fust, convinced that Gutenberg was wasting time and money, sued him in court. In 1452, the judge ruled in favor of Fust and Gutenberg lost all his possessions including his tools.

By the time the Gutenberg Bible was published around 1455 or 1456, Gutenberg, who had done most of the work, was no longer in charge of the production process. Fust continued the printing using the equipment that Gutenberg had developed, but Gutenberg was forced to begin again. Warfare in 1462 destroyed the Fust printing plant and other printers left Mainz. Gutenberg stayed, but his poverty required him to request a salary and privileges for services rendered. He obtained a sinecure in 1465 and he continued to print. Because he did not identify his works, it's difficult to definitely determine his ownership of the products which he printed. Before he died in 1468, he is believed to have gone blind. He was buried on the grounds of a convent which was later demolished.

If his most famous creation is the printing press, his most celebrated product is the Gutenberg Bible, 200 copies of which were printed at some point between 1450-1455. Today it's estimated that even a single two-sided page from an original Bible is worth $100,000, making his work the rarest printed material in the world.

Painting in Renaissance Germany

Hans Holbein, the father and the son (distinguished as the Elder and the Younger) were important figures in the German painting arena. Holbein the Elder, along with his brother, are seen as the navigators who steered German Gothic art to the new Renaissance style. Holbein the Younger painted portraits, but artists traveled to earn their living and his talents were put to use not in Germany but in England and Switzerland. Holbein the Younger's woodcuts on the Dance of Death were part of a series produced by a group of printmakers known as the Little Masters, whose small, detailed engravings were a favorite of collectors. Some of the subjects of the works by the Little Masters depicted erotic rather than religious subjects, another indication of the way in which secular interests were gaining ground during the Renaissance.

Engraving in Renaissance Germany

Printmaking by the use of woodcuts and engraving had originated in China, but the expansion of trade and travel brought Chinese innovations to Europe and the Germans were in the forefront of developing illustrations for books. The quality was not particularly high, but the illustrations enjoyed a mass audience because the woodblocks were often lent to the printers in other cities. The new field had become so attractive that the German artist Michael

Wolgemut left painting behind to focus on the new art form. When his Nuremberg workshop accepted Albrecht Durer as an apprentice, engraving was about to recognize a master.

RENAISSANCE MAN: Albrecht Dürer

Durer learned his trade under Wolgemut and his apprenticeship came to an end in 1490 when he was around the age of 19. He then spent some years traveling in Germany, followed by a few months in Italy. When he returned to Nuremberg, he was ready to set up his own workshop and Europe was ready for his talent. His woodcuts and engravings, which showed his German influence but also displayed nuances of the Italian style, became famous all across the Continent. So distinctive was his style that it's regarded as representative of the German rendition of Renaissance visual arts, supplanting France and the Netherlands for the ensuing 40 years as the most innovative art in Northern Europe. Durer was also a painter and, although a supporter of Reformation pioneer Martin Luther, used traditional religious topics as inspiration for his art.

Faith and art had to find safe ground for expression, and not all artists and thinkers of the Renaissance would be as fortunate as Durer.

Chapter Six

The Low Countries Renaissance

The regions known as the Low Countries include what we today call the Netherlands, Belgium, and French Flanders. These countries in Europe endured a different sense of nationhood that affected their geographical boundaries and their independence. This region, a thriving conduit for trade, was familiar with the evolving changes in Italy which were the result of the Renaissance. Commerce which made the Low Countries wealthy would also help to make them creative.

Burgundy was the inheritance of a younger branch of the French royal house of Valois. But in 1477 the Valois line died out and the duchy reverted to France. The Austrian Hapsburgs felt that they were entitled to some of the lucrative lands, and the result was war in 1479. The disputed territory of Artois was renounced by the French king, which led to Philip the Handsome gaining Artois and Flanders. Philip's marriage to Juana of Castile brought the Spanish into the mix; their son Charles V would be the heir to the largest empire in the world and the Netherlands would end up under the control of a foreign power.

By the time the 16th century reached its end, Northern and Southern Netherlands were divided; Spain maintained control over the southern region and the Dutch Republic in the north became a commercial powerhouse, with a fleet of merchant ships that was larger than that of any other nation. The Dutch prowess at trade led to the creation, in 1602, of what is the world's oldest stock exchange.

Creativity does not hinge on prosperity, but it does benefit when a region's economy is going well. This success fueled the Renaissance in the region knows as the Low Countries. Religious division did not benefit the region; the Reformation led to religious warfare even though philosophers such as Erasmus of Rotterdam, despite his criticism of its practices, remained loyal to the Catholic Church. The Low Countries began to embrace Protestantism but Spain could not tolerate humanism, which it regarded as heresy. While the northern region became the Dutch Republic and Protestant, the Spanish set the Counter-Reformation in the southern region.

RENAISSANCE MAN: Peter Brueghel

Like their counterparts in Italy, the wealthy nobles of the Low Countries could afford to commission the cream of the artist crop. Peter Brueghel, whose painting skills would continue into subsequent generations through the talents of his sons, was born in the Netherlands in 1525. He was apprenticed to Pieter Coecke van Aelst, a sculptor, architect, and artist based in Antwerp whose influences showed the effects of his travels to Turkey and Italy. An artist's technique revealed his itinerary; when Brueghel went on his own travels, he made his way to Rome to work with Giulio Clovio, an artist who had been influenced by Michelangelo.

In 1563, Brueghel married the daughter of his master. He owed more than his spouse to his in-laws. From his mother-in-law, Maria Verhulst Bessemers, also an artist, he became familiar with the technique known as tempera, which employed the suspension of pigments in a glutinous substance such as egg yolks on linen.

Brueghel died in 1569, but his sons Jan and Pieter the Younger continued the tradition of painting and the Brueghels would remain an artistic dynasty into the 18th century.

Science in the Low Countries Renaissance

National nomenclature for people of the Low Countries depended upon timing. For Renaissance stand-out Andreas Vesalius, who was born in 1514 in what is today Brussels, Belgium, his homeland was part of the Holy Roman Empire. Vesalius, a third-generation physician, studied medicine in Paris but had to leave his studies when the Holy Roman Empire declared war on France. After continuing his studies at the University of Louvain and then in Padua, he was offered the chair of surgery and anatomy when his studies were complete in 1537.

It's hard to understand now, but in that time, knowledge of surgery and anatomy were not regarded as priorities for physicians. Vesalius, however, was convinced that a foundation in knowledge of anatomy was crucial in the medical field. Because Vesalius was knowledgeable about the circulatory system, he was able to offer an informed opinion regarding blood-letting, then a popular remedy for illness, and from what area of the body the blood should be taken. Vesalius' experience came from the dissections he performed, which enabled him to create anatomical charts of the circulatory and nervous systems as references for students.

In 1539, a judge in Padua presented Vesalius with an opportunity to expand his anatomical expertise when he offered him the bodies of criminals who'd been executed so that he could perform dissections which allowed him to compare his findings. When he published De Humani Corporis Fabrica in 1543, he presented anatomy as a subject that was based on primary research from dissections he had done and his observations of his findings. At this time, he, following the family tradition, became the physician first for the Emperor Charles V, and then for his son, Philip II of Spain. He had left anatomical research behind for his medical practice but his contributions to the field transformed the study of anatomy. Vesalius died in 1564 when he was en route to a trip to the Holy Land.

RENAISSANCE MAN: Gerard Mercator

Born in 1511, Gerard Mercator was the son of a shoemaker and his wife who struggled to provide for his family. But the parents valued education; an older son had been educated at Louvain University and served in the priesthood. When the family moved from Mercator's birthplace in Gangelt to Rupelmonde, Gerard was able to attend school where he studied arithmetic, Latin, and religion. The Reformation and the warfare that ensued, however, rerouted any plans the family might have had for Gerard to enter the priesthood; when the father died in 1526 or 1527, his brother Gilbert became his guardian. Gilbert sent him to be educated in the Netherlands. When a student, Mercator changed his surname from Kremer, which meant merchant, to Mercator, the Latin word for merchant. His new name was Gerardus Mercator de Rupelmonde.

Although he graduated from Louvain University with a Master's Degree based on studies of Aristotle, he was no longer convinced that the Church-sanctioned Aristotelian teachings were accurate. He was also troubled by the inconsistencies regarding the Creation of the universe as it was presented in the Bible. What does a bright young student do when faced with intellectual quandaries? He travels. And so Mercator left the university and discovered geography, which allowed him to avoid a crisis of faith while exploring a field to its depths. When he returned to the university in 1534, he studied mathematics that applied to cosmography. Mercator with the help of his instructor was able to progress in his studies, applying mathematics to geography and astronomy. He earned money as a tutor in mathematics, as well as selling mathematical instruments which he made.

Chapter Seven

The English Renaissance

The island nation emerged from the Middle Ages later than some of the other nations, with its Renaissance beginning around 1520, and ending approximately a century later in 1620. It would be convenient to begin the English rebirth in 1485, when the Plantagenet dynasty came to an end at Bosworth Field with the death of Richard III and the rise of the Tudors, but England's flowering came under the reign of Elizabeth I, the granddaughter of the first Henry Tudor and daughter of Henry VIII, whose quest for a male heir turned England from a Catholic to a Protestant nation, a switch which would have a dramatic effect when the English began to settle in the New World.

England was still a rural nation during the Renaissance, but London became one of Europe's most populated cities, its numbers doubling to 200,000 as the city became a trade center. Centuries later, the Emperor Napoleon would describe England as a nation of shopkeepers. The English did take to commerce in their own fashion. England's expansion into commerce led to the development of The Muscovy Company, which saw an expedition heading to Moscow in 1553 to develop a monopoly on Russian trade. Expanding trade was a driving force in the Renaissance and England was eager to profit from new commercial contacts.

Music and Art in Renaissance England

Unlike the grand visual arts explosion of the Italian Renaissance, the English made their mark in the fields of music and literature. While England did cultivate some artists, they were often imported; for instance, Hans Holbein, the Flemish painter, one of whose portraits was commissioned by none other than that marrying man, Henry VIII, left his homeland to paint. The practice of portrait miniatures, which were small paintings worn in lockets, was an English innovation that proved to be popular.

Music in England, particularly the madrigal, was one of the areas in which the Renaissance influence was visible. The madrigal had its roots in Italy and was a popular form of music throughout Europe, but only in England did the tradition develop roots. A large collection of Italian madrigals was published in 1588 by Nicholas Yonge. Thomas Morely understood the Italian format and adapted it to English tastes, which included light poetry and music.

In literature and drama, England took center stage. The English already had a literary tradition beginning with Beowulf from its Anglo-Saxon days. William Langland's Piers Plowman and Thomas Malory's Le Morte D'Arthur attested to a strong tradition in England for literature. Geoffrey Chaucer in the Late Middle Ages, with his Canterbury Tales, brought forth a full-bodied work of literature which displayed a keen perception of human nature. William Shakespeare, who went to London as a young man and became an actor and playwright, brought an equally shrewd understanding of men and women to the page. When Shakespeare arrived in London, Christopher Marlowe and Thomas Kyd were already established as playwrights. But the man who would be known as the Bard of Avon was destined to recalibrate the dramatic tradition.

RENAISSANCE MAN: William Shakespeare

The man whose literary talent set the bar so high that perhaps no other dramatist has been able to meet it was born in 1564 of fairly humble origins in Stratford-on-Avon, the son of a glover and a woman whose family had some claim to local prosperity. He may have had some schooling, but he would later be derided by his London rivals for his lack of pedigree. He was married at 18 to the 26-year old Anne Hathaway who was already pregnant when the vows were made. A daughter was born, and then twins. The next seven years of his life, Shakespeare's lost years, are the subject of speculation: was he in hiding because he had been caught poaching? Was he working as a schoolmaster? What is known is that, sometime in the 1580s, he arrived in London. By 1592, he was earning a living as a playwright and actor, and was successful enough to stir up resentment among his contemporaries, one of whom, Robert Greene, wrote that Shakespeare, in his own conceit, considered himself the only "Shaks-scene in a country." By the end of the decade, he was a partner in the Lord Chamberlain's Men acting company. Although theatre was very popular, it was not regarded as a gentlemanly pursuit, and Shakespeare's poetry was more genteel, enabling him to dedicate his poems The Rape of Lucrece and Venus and Adonis to Henry Wriothesley, the Earl of Southampton. Prosperity favored him and he was able to purchase property in his hometown which served as an investment.

Poets such as Thomas Wyatt and Edmund Spenser were renowned for their skills, but here again, Shakespeare held his own. The plays of Shakespeare and his contemporaries reflected the worldly imprint of the Renaissance, rather than the pious, influence of the past, when the brand of faith was replaced by humanism, and the knowledge of people as they were in their daily lives rather than when they were at their prayers.

Religion in Renaissance England

England underwent its religious division before it entered the Renaissance, to its experience did not depend on the accessibility of reading material from Germany. England, since Henry VIII had split from Rome and declared himself the head of the Church, had been seesawing between Catholic and Protestant religious turmoil. Henry was Protestant because it was the only way he could obtain a divorce from his Catholic wife. His heir, Edward VI, was a firm Protestant during whose reign The Book of Common Prayer was produced. The Book of Common Prayer helped to create a sense of tradition in the Anglican faith despite its rough-hewn origins.

Mary, the daughter that Henry and his Catholic wife Katherine had, was a committed Catholic who returned the English to the faith of her heritage during her reign. By the time Elizabeth I, a Protestant who had seen enough of religious division, took the throne, the country was torn. She sought to bring stability during her reign; Protestantism was the religion of the country, but Elizabeth was not a zealot.

England's switch to a Protestant creed would bring about two works of literature with an enduring legacy. King James I, who succeeded Queen Elizabeth in 1603, wanted a Bible that was accurate in its translation from Latin, and uniform in its theology. What he received was a work that blended poetry with scholarship: The King James Version of the Bible has sustained members of the Protestant faith centuries after its publication.

RENAISSANCE MAN: Thomas Tallis

The arts would to some extent reflect the pendulum of religious thought which characterized the country. A composer who symbolized this religious dichotomy, Thomas Tallis, was born early in the 16th century, perhaps in 1505. He would live under four monarchs; his music would outlast the dissension of faith during his lifetime.

He may have been a choirboy, perhaps one of the children of the Chapel Royal, where many composers of his time learned music. In 5132, he was appointed the organist for Dover's Benedictine Priory. He was employed by other religious institutions until King Henry's dissolution of the monasteries which began in 1540. He then became a lay clerk in 1541 at Canterbury Cathedral. In 1543 he was named a Gentleman of the Chapel Royal, working for the King, where he sang, played the organ, worked with the choir, and composed music. To survive and thrive in an era of conflict and religious upheaval, a musician had to be both talented and flexible. Gaude Gloriosa was believed to have been composed in honor of Queen Mary I, the Catholic monarch. When writing for a Catholic monarchy, he used vocal polyphony to set Latin texts to music. When the music was needed for a Protestant monarch and the Church of England, his choral settings used English texts.

His well-known Tallis' Canon is still used today by church choirs, confirming his reputation as England's major composer of church music. He was able to secure a monopoly on printing music and music paper in England in 1575 along with his pupil and protégé William Byrd. His composition Spem in alium was said to have been written in response to a challenge by the Duke of Howard, a Catholic, to find an Englishman who could produce a composition that would surpass the 40-part Ecce beatam lautan by Striggio. When Tallis performed his work, the Duke of Norfolk acknowledged that the challenge had been met and he placed a gold chain of his possession around Talllis' neck.

Chapter Eight

Here Be Dragons: Exploring the Unknown

Here be dragons. That simple phrase could have defined the medieval era, a time when fear of the unknown was a reason to hover close to what was familiar, unchallenged, and safe. But the Renaissance didn't cower from what was new, untried, or unfamiliar. In painting, politics, architecture, literature, music, technology, and even religion, new frontiers awaited the advent of the bold who were willing to blaze new trails.

It's impossible to fully understand the liberation of thought which ushered in the thinking that characterized the Renaissance. Unfettered by the fears that had gripped their forefathers, Renaissance thinkers, artists, merchants, theologians and inventors all across Europe believed in the capacity of their own mortal nature to learn and to do. As a result, men and women of the Renaissance often found themselves at odds with the prevailing religious authorities who distrusted ideas which had not been pre-tested and given the papal seal of approval. But unlocking doors was a character trait of the Renaissance that neither the hope of heaven nor the fear of hell could shackle.

That spirit of adventure was seen in the alacrity with which European nations set sail for a world they had never seen. They put to sea to find gold and spices, but what they found were lands that were unknown to them, inhabited by people who were very different. Colonization would not always reflect well on the Europeans who landed, but that dark story, while it must never be forgotten, is separate from the saga of the brave sailors who left familiar shores to find out what was out there, and to prove that dragons were not waiting for them.

The nation of Portugal was an early leader in navigation thanks to the enthusiasm of Prince Henry, who promoted the building of a lighter ship, the easy-to-maneuver caravel, which was able to sail with speed. The Portuguese began to explore Africa's Atlantic coast beginning in 1418. Portugal sent Vasco da Gama to India, which he reached by sailing around Africa. Da Gama managed to open up direct trade routes with Asia. Shortly after, Portuguese sailors were able to refute the claim that sea monsters were waiting at the end of the world when they reached Cape Bojador in 1434.

Spain sent Christopher Columbus from Genoa to cross the Atlantic and find the Indies; instead, Columbus found the Americas. Spain sent another explorer, this time Ferdinand Magellan of Portugal to explore, and he circumnavigated the globe. Other Spanish explorers who left the home shores to search for gold and lands included Francisco Pizarro, Hernan Cortés, Vasco Núñez de Balboa and others. Spanish ships bringing the wealth of the conquered lands helped to make Spain a mighty empire.

Dutch sailing ships joined the nautical competition in 1495, sailing the Pacific Ocean around the South American continent and later discovering Australia and New Zealand. The exploration of Siberia occupied Russia for decades, beginning in the 1580s, and by 1640s, they had conquered the vast region.

Giovanni Caboto of Venice, or John Cabot as he is familiarly known, was sent in 1497 by Henry VIII to cross the Atlantic to find a route to the trade routes of Asia. Those trade routes did not emerge, but English colonization of North America would in time contribute to the power of what would become, in another century, the British Empire.

Francis I of France sent Giovanni da Verrazzano of Genoa to venture across the Atlantic; the quest led him to Canada, which he claimed in the name of the French king.

In time, the Dutch, French, Spanish, and English would battle for supremacy of the lands their explorers had discovered. Empires would rise and fall, new countries would be born, but the expanded landscape of the known world had its roots in the free-thinking air of the Renaissance.

The willingness to challenge the status quo and explore unknown worlds that characterized the Renaissance mindset was not merely intellectual, as these names prove. Nations, Protestant and Catholic alike, were inspired to tread on new soil. A new age, born out of the freedom of thought of the Renaissance, was on the horizon, and its appeal and influence would spread to those new lands.

CPSIA information can be obtained
at www.ICGtesting.com
Printed in the USA
LVOW08s0337021116
511207LV00018B/2018/P